Always

MW00998136

ISBN-10:1517212871

ISBN-13:978-1517212872

Unless otherwise indicated all scriptures are taken from the
New King James version of the Bible.

hisbest4usorders@gmail.com

Printed in USA by HIS Best Publishing

Table of Contents

Chapter 1   Prayer

Everywhere I travel, I am asked to email and text the prayers I pray while in fellowship with believers. It's not 'easy' because the LORD helps me identify the exact needs and words while I am praying with people for their situations or praying with them on behalf of issues their friends and family members are facing.

Finally, after so many requests, I agreed to prepare a prayer pamphlet. However, my plan became Chapter 10 in *A Wake Up Call: It's Restoration Time!* Trusted it would be enough. However, the LORD prompted so many people to ask me for more. Then, He provided examples & confirmed the title through three complete strangers: *You always speak life. I've never prayed like you pray.*

The credit goes to our LORD because prayer is personal and our personal relationship with Him makes all the difference.

The LORD prompted me to insert the LORD's prayer which Christ gave to us. I resisted because I inserted the prayer in prior books. The LORD was serious. He told me I did not do a complete job. I asked what was missing. He confirmed many who say they believe do not know who they are praying to when they pray.

Shocked, so the LORD prompted me to Google the names of Baal. Hard to think I would be so bold in the moment with the LORD but, I actually told the LORD: *Baal is ancient worship.* He was gentle with me when He merely responded, *He is current.*

Deeply humbled after I repented and Googled to find the names of Baal: God, Lord and Master. Plus, they are in capital letters. After a time of tears sitting with the LORD at my computer screen, I asked what I could share to bless the people beyond the LORD's prayer. He prompted me to insert *Hallowed Be Thy Name* so the people would know who they are praying to and they would learn His true names, character and nature.

Hallowed be Thy Name

Hallowed be Thy name. I bless Your name, Elohim, the Creator of heaven and earth, who was in the beginning. It is You Who made me, and You have crowned me with glory and honor. You are the God of might and strength.

Hallowed be Thy name. I bless Your name, El-Shaddai, the God Almighty of blessings. Your are the one who nourishes and supplies. You are all-bountiful and all sufficient.

Hallowed be Thy name. I bless Your name, Adonai, my Lord and my Master. You are Jehovah – the completely self-existing one, always present, revealed in Jesus who is the same yesterday, today and forever.

Hallowed be Thy name. I bless Your name, Jehovah-Jireh, the one who sees my needs and provides for them.

Hallowed be Thy name. I bless Your name, Jehovah-Rapha, my healer and the one who makes bitter experiences sweet. You sent Your word and healed me. You forgive all my iniquities and You healed all my diseases.

Hallowed be Thy name. I bless Your name, Jehovah-M'Kaddesh, the Lord my sanctifier. You have set me apart for Yourself.

Hallowed be Thy name. Jehovah-Nissi, You are my victory, my banner and my Standard. Your banner over me is love. When the enemy shall come in like a flood, You will lift up a standard against him.

Hallowed be Thy name. Jehovah-Shalom, I bless Your Name. You are my Peace – the peace which transcends all understanding, which garrisons and mounts guard over my heart and mind in Christ Jesus, my Yeshua HaMashiach.

Hallowed be Thy name. I bless you, Jehovah-Tsidkenu, my righteousness. Thank You for sending Your Son to become sin for me that I might become the righteousness of God in Christ Jesus.

Hallowed be Thy name. Jehovah-Rohi, You are my shepherd and I shall not want for any good or beneficial thing.

Hallowed be Thy name. Hallelujah to Jehovah-Shammah Who will never leave me or forsake me. You are always there. I take comfort and am encouraged as I confidently and boldly say, the Lord is my Helper, I will not be seized with alarm. I will not fear or dread or be terrified. What can man do to me?

Hallowed be Thy name. I worship and adore You, El-Elyon, the Most High God Who is the first cause of everything, the possessor of the heavens and earth. You are the everlasting God, the great-God, the living God, the merciful-God, the faithful-God, the mighty-God. You are truth, justice, righteousness and perfection. You are El-Elyon – the highest Sovereign of the heavens and the earth. Hallowed be Thy name.

Powerful. Tearful to realize the truth. This is the truth when we come to our Savior and pray in His name, our Jesus Christ, our Yeshua Hamashiach and we claim our salvation for the truth is the Father and the Son are one with the Holy Spirit communicating to and working through us, guiding us when we praise our LORD is our Jehovah, our Elohim, our Adonai, and He resides in the praises of His people!

Chapter 2   The Model Prayer

Now, I can reveal what the LORD did not let me reveal within *A Wake Up Call: It's Restoration Time!*

When I asked the LORD how I could explain the insert of *Hallowed Be Thy Name,* He prompted to say it came from a bible scholar. So, that is what I stated in the book because He told me that we listen to bible scholars more often than we listen Him.

Wow. May we turn from our wicked ways, seek His truth and align with His will and plan for our lives by obeying Him so our LORD will reign over our lives and our situations.

The Model Prayer

Matthew 6:5-14. The Model Prayer. And when you pray, you shall not be like the hypocrites. For they love to pray standing in the synagogues and on the corners of the streets, that they may be seen by men. Assuredly, I say to you, they have their reward.

⁶ But <u>you, when you pray, go into your room, and when you have shut your door, pray to your Father who *is* in the secret *place;* and your Father who sees in secret will reward you openly.</u>

⁷ And <u>when you pray, do not use vain repetitions as the heathen *do,* for they think that they will be heard for their many words.</u>

⁸ <u>Therefore do not be like them. For your Father knows the things you have need of before you ask Him.</u> ⁹ In this manner, therefore, pray:

Our Father in heaven, Hallowed be Your name.

¹⁰ Your kingdom come.

Your will be done

On earth as *it is* in heaven.

¹¹ Give us this day our daily bread.

¹² And forgive us our debts,

As we forgive our debtors.

¹³ And do not lead us into temptation,

But deliver us from the evil one.

For Yours is the kingdom and the power and the glory forever.

Amen.

[14] *For if you forgive men their trespasses, your heavenly Father will also forgive you.*

[15] But *if you do not forgive men their trespasses, neither will your Father forgive your trespasses.*

It is powerful to pray this prayer each morning until prayer becomes part of a personal and deep relationship with the LORD.

The time together becomes a special time which nothing else during the day can replace.

Philippians 4:5-7. Rejoice in the Lord always. Again I will say, rejoice! [5] Let your gentleness be known to all men.

The Lord *is* at hand.

[6] Be anxious for nothing, but in everything by prayer and supplication, with thanksgiving, let your requests be made known to God;

[7] and the peace of God, which surpasses all understanding, will guard your hearts and minds through Christ Jesus.

Feeling Like A Kick-Start to Life is Required?

Remember: There are no levels of membership within the body of Christ! The LORD loves each of us the exact same amount.

May we each remain humble servants of our true Adonai.

We learn as much as we can, as fast as we are willing to learn.

What is required?

The willingness to change. A good start to this process is our willingness to conform our mind to the mind of our Savior, Christ! Otherwise, are we truly a Christian?

The LORD took me from being a pew warming Scandinavian Lutheran to being a representative of Yeshua Hamashiach globally while training me 'on site' each step of the way.

Reminder: He loves you! He really, really loves you! He will do for you what He has done for me and for other believers over the decades and He will never forsake you so enjoy your private time with Him each day and share your heart with him each time you pray.

Chapter 3   Power In Prayer

The LORD Introduced Me To Bishop McKinney

The LORD placed my feet on nearly every continent and no matter where it was or what language was being spoken, everywhere I went the people told me about Bishop McKinney.

During a major rainstorm, a man called from Los Angeles to tell me he was on his way to San Diego for a board meeting with Bishop McKinney and he would introduce us, if I was available.

Excited about the miracle. The LORD arranged for Bishop McKinney to be in San Diego and I was finally going to meet him.

Limited parking near the address provided. One spot was available in front of the building.

A man motioned for me to take the parking place but, I knew someone attending the meeting with Bishop McKinney would need that parking space, so I waved to acknowledge him while I drove around the building two more times.

The next time, the man was in the street and motioned me to the parking spot so I rolled down the passenger window a bit to let him know I will only be needing a spot for a few minutes but, there are important people coming for a board meeting with Bishop McKinney and they will need the spot in front of the building. The man merely smiled and motioned me into the parking place.

For months, out of loyalty of being a pew warming Lutheran for a few decades, I attended a Lutheran church at 8 AM, twenty miles from an Assembly of God church I attended at 10 AM. Every week I asked the LORD where I could fellowship with people who understand me so I would finally have a church home.

The moment the man standing in the rain took my hand between his, he said: ***For the LORD would have you know, I'm Bishop McKinney, I understand you and you have a home here.***

Speechless. It was a unique moment in my life.

I tried to talk to him. I really, really tried to talk but, my words turned to mush as they started to leave my mouth. It was embarrassing but, he did not appear to notice. Instead, he kept confirming truth to me, while I uttered parts of words or mainly the sounds. Seriously, what was coming out of my mouth sounded to me like just a series of odd sounds.

Bishop brought ·clarity to everything by handing me his card while telling me to call his secretary and set up an appointment in three days. Tears so I was not able to read his card or see the San Diego address.

No sleep for me the next three nights.

While I sat at my computer, I asked the LORD what I should share in the introductory letter for Bishop. The LORD merely responded, each time, with the simple phrase: *Tell him what happened when I sent you ...when I introduced you to ...*

The LORD was not done until moments prior to the meeting. While the pages were printing, I had just enough time to jump in the shower and wash my hair but, not one minute to dry it or style it, so I merely grabbed some combs in an attempt to put my hair in place. It was worth it, because I arrived at the appointed time.

When I met with Bishop, I handed him the stack of pages which comprised the total summary of events the LORD wanted me to add to my introductory letter. He smiled, turned the pages over on his desk, placed his hand on the pages and began praying.

He started from the beginning and prayed through the entire letter. I did not identify any of the people or the ministries but, Bishop knew each one and included them within the prayer. It was a complete surprise, a first experience for me.

I did not identify the men's ministry. Bishop thanked me for helping Promise Keepers. I said it's in there but, I did not say it was Promise Keepers. He's the chaplain. He knew...

I did not identify the man crowned king in Africa but, Bishop thanked me for being God's witness. Again, I said: *It's in there but I did not identify the person.* Bishop said he was supposed to go as a witness and Kingsley Fletcher is his friend of a few years but, Bishop was not able to attend so he is glad the LORD sent me.

Then, Bishop asked me about Bishop Duncan Williams. I was stunned and could not think why the name sounded familiar or how I would know the name when Bishop smiled and said how much Bishop Williams enjoyed meeting me in Africa. Bishop McKinney and Bishop Williams serve together on the board of Morris Cerrulo and Billy Graham, I believe.

Bishop advised me to add the facts, the names of the people and the ministries, within the text so I did and my introductory letter became the content of the first book: ***It's A Faith Walk!***

Night after night I asked the LORD how I could receive answers to my prayers as Bishop McKinney received the answers.

The LORD Introduced Me To Harald Bredesen

While attending Bishop McKinney's Sunday service the LORD introduced me to a special guest, Pastor Harald Bredesen.

Clearly, the LORD was answering my prayer because He decided to speed up the process with me by introducing me to a saved, sanctified, delivered and set free, spirit-filled Lutheran pastor, Harald Bredesen (1918-2006).

So special amongst believers! He is dearly missed.

He was an amazing man of God, a mighty disciple who fully expressed the five-fold ministry.

He was unique for he was allowed to remain in his career as a Lutheran pastor after he became spirit-filled.

Harald is credited with founding the Charismatic Movement globally. He served on the boards of many top international ministries, with a deep friendship for many decades with Pat Robertson at CBN to being on the board of Benny Hinn.

Every moment with Harald was filled with God's wisdom.

He prayed without ceasing, during every moment in his presence: ***"Thank you, Jesus, praise you, LORD ..."***

During each moment I was blessed to be in the presence of the LORD with Harald (it is the best way I can describe the experience as it was powerful each and every second), I could easily hear the soft whispers as he praised the LORD and thanked Christ with every breath.

His life was absolutely the full expression of being a spirit-filled, guided and directed man of God.

Anyone who spent time with him heard him whisper, pray, praise and worship the LORD constantly while thanking Christ.

Everything the LORD was doing through me, everything about me (the good, the bad & the ugly) was given to Harald from the

LORD during our first meeting. The LORD gave Harald the 'inside scoop' and it was amazing to witness!

Example: Harald knew me and introduced me to key pastors throughout the region before we met in person.

Example: Harald told CBN's 700 Club representative locally all about me while Harald did not share the fact he was on the CBN board, he shared a prophecy which changed the location or identified the exact location for the studio.

Example: Harald knew I experienced Identity Theft. He was taken advantage of and the LORD told him I would know how to help him before he knew anything about me or my situation(s).

Example: Harald arranged with Benny Hinn for me to be interviewed, before Harald knew anything about me or my ministry in the natural. After everything was prepared for my interview, TBN called & sent Dr. Nasir Siddiki to the studio for Benny to interview. The LORD shifted my purpose in attending the taping to be His witness. I became the ONLY witness to the prophetic word Pastor Benny stated during a prior TV program about a Muslim converting and bringing the testimony and his name would be Nasir.

Bishop McKinney and Harald Bredesen knew something I did not know. Clearly, what they knew was something I had never learned. The relationship they have with the LORD made me hungry for a deeper relationship.

Help Me Be More Like You, LORD!

Psalms 22:3-5. *But You are holy, enthroned in the praises of Israel. [4] Our fathers trusted in You; They trusted, and You delivered them. [5] They cried to You, and were delivered; They trusted in You, and were not ashamed.*

Come together with prayer warriors who know how to pray and seek the LORD's truth for it is powerful to experience the LORD's orchestration of the details once the prayer is spoken and all involved await the LORDs report, the testimony which will cause us and those who are not filled with faith to become filled with faith and strengthened for our daily walk!

Matthew 18:20. *For where two or three are gathered together in My name, I am there in the midst of them."*

Call upon Him for He is great and greatly to be praised!

Once you gain a relationship with the LORD you will desire to be in fellowship with Him throughout the day and the night.

We often hear the first half of the verse while there is great meaning in the second part of the verse: **James 4:8.** *Draw near to*

God and He will draw near to you. <u>Cleanse your hands, you sinners; and purify your hearts, you double-minded</u>.

Becoming Saved, Sanctified, Delivered and Free is important.

Time with the LORD in prayer renews our strength, helps us to run and not be weary. The entire chapter 40 in Isaiah confirms the LORD comforts His people. The last verse is often shared and it explains our pray life with out LORD, seeking His will, His truth for each decision and choice as we progress through our day(s):

Isaiah 40:31.

> But those who wait on the Lord
> Shall renew *their* strength;
> They shall mount up with wings like eagles,
> They shall run and not be weary,
> They shall walk and not faint.

Chapter 4   Answered Prayer

All believers have the same opportunity to pray and receive answers to prayer.

Prayer begins with relationship. Being in relationship with the Father, the Son and the Holy Spirit and having reverence for the one true living LORD changes things!

When we seek and want 'answers' that align with our requests, we are not praying for the LORD's will to be done on earth as it is in heaven!

Well-meaning believers have often said: *"Adding the Son's name is supposed to make it happen. The scriptures say whatever you ask for in the Son's name it will be granted."*

However, the rest of the scripture is typically ignored.

John 14:13-14. And whatever you ask in My name, that I will do, that the Father may be glorified in the Son. [14] If you ask anything in My name, I will do *it.*

So, does your prayer request glorify the Father in the Son?

Or, is the prayer request all about self needs, wants & desires.

Christ provided the best prayer example.

The powerful structure covers all categories, honoring our heavenly Father as the LORD of all, seeking His kingdom, His will, on earth as it is in heaven, His provision, His forgiveness, confirming our forgiveness of others (and, be sure to ask the Father to help you forgive you!), His protection against temptation, His deliverance from evil, knowing it is His kingdom and His power granted to us so we might be in His glory with Him & the Son forever.

Wow. What could be more important than praying this prayer each day?

The results are amazing when this prayer is prayed daily!

None of the members in the body are loved more or have a higher position with the LORD for He loves all of His children.

Why am I mentioning this fact regarding prayer?

Many people trust other believers get all the answers because they have a closer connection with the LORD because their prayers appear to be answered quicker or more often. The focus may need to shift within us so we spend more time in relationship with the LORD and therefore our prayer life is richer and then it may appear to other believers that our prayers are answered quicker or more often as we enter into a personal, deep conversation and relationship with the LORD. We become willing to humble ourselves, turn from our wicked ways, seek Him & hear His truth

The Answered Prayer

We often see part of a scripture as a quote: *"If you ask anything in My name, I will do it"*

Perhaps this is how the body of Christ focused upon asking, asking, asking and expecting!

Believers quote this partial truth which is not the whole truth. In fact, the quote is on posters, T-shirts, etc. However, whatever we ask Christ to do should be something for which the Father will be glorified in the Son.

John 14: 12-14. "Most assuredly, I say to you, he who believes in Me, the works that I do he will do also; and greater works than these he will do, because I go to My Father. [13] And whatever you

ask in My name, that I will do, that the Father may be glorified in the Son. [14] If you ask anything in My name, I will do it."

Seek & Find; Knock & It Shall Be Opened Unto You

We took this scripture (in Matthew & Luke) to be the 'method' and we've been hammering it each and every day, since. **Example:** What would your reaction be if a child asked you each day for the same toy they wanted from the same store, and every day they remind you about a toy you did not purchase yet?

Yikes. This is what repetitive, ritual prayer sounds like!

Nobody gave me another perspective about prayer!

So, I kept asking and reminding! Not good.

But, well-meaning people said, *"Prayers of the righteous avail much."* I did not see anything my prayers were availing!

What happened? I prayed what I heard other people pray.

They kept asking God to do everything for them, so I made a checklist of everything I wanted God to do for me.

I prayed for the same things day after day after day.

My thoughts took me right down the slippery slope into hope deferred! Not wanting to remember how long I sat there!

Repeatedly, I asked the LORD to do what I wanted Him to do! And, after hearing the prayers of the church leaders, I used their same 'method' of praying.

Seriously, I was merely updating God each day on how well He was doing on the long list of everything I wanted Him to do for me. Then, I concluded the prayer by reviewing the list of everything He had not told me He was taking care of for me, yet.

No relationship with the LORD was evident. I did not know how to be in a relationship with Him. So, I clearly had no understanding of how to be with the LORD and be in prayer personally with Him. I will never forget the day when our LORD merely asked me: *"Do you trust Me?"* I thought I did. However, He confirmed less than 100% is not trust. I stopped pleading and started trusting!

Is our LORD is enough in your life? Is He all-sufficient?

Trust God is enough. Become aware of any words, thoughts or actions which confirm in your heart & mind, and to other people that God is not enough in your life … any area where you 'fill in' is exactly where you think God left a hole in the plan. Truth is truth!

This 'homework' may help.

List 7-10 things the LORD has done for you lately.

1.

2.

3.

4.

5.

6.

7.

8.

9.

10.

Do Not Lean on Human Understanding

The LORD knew I was experiencing some extreme circumstances in the world. I trusted key leaders 'in authority' as they were 'in charge' and they were extremely successful, a fact I learned to admire because I was told again and again, the more successful someone is, the closer to God they are in their faith walk. However, it was not known that they were not men of God. When people operate in their own power, albeit they appear on the surface to be very successful, they do not know how to operate within God's power and authority and their advice is not going to improve the circumstances.

After the LORD revealed the men were not to be accepted as counsel, He reminded me of the many times He took my hand and brought me through situations which would have destroyed me.

Only the LORD Can Do What the LORD Does

The LORD directed my path to powerful prayer warriors, people filled with the Holy Spirit, people who were experiencing divine orchestration of their daily details. A few examples of the powerful men & women of God who proved the LORD is in charge: **The LORD introduced me to: Bishop McKinney, Pastor Harald Bredesen, and then, to Rodney Howard-Browne.**

Pastor Mark Spitzbergen arranged for Rodney Howard-Browne to be in San Diego on a fairly regular schedule.

Example: The first time I attended a meeting, the LORD launched me forth and I was not home very much (beyond, re-packing for the next assignment) the next three years.

Example: Another night, I was given a last minute ride to a meeting. The LORD reminded me to 'take the scarves' I sell when I speak. The LORD arranged for me to sell exactly the number of scarves required for the transportation I needed to get to the next assignment. It was an assignment I had no knowledge of prior to the meeting, and yet, I quickly packed that night and departed on a shuttle for an international flight early the next morning.

Example: The LORD orchestrated a meeting between a station manager of a Christian Television Network studio who stated his launch into ministry was inspired during a Rodney Howard Browne meeting. The Pastor in the region who was meeting with us confirmed his ministry was launched during a meeting with Rodney Howard-Browne while he was in college at Oral Roberts University.

And then, to Kathryn Kuhlman, Rex Humbard, John G Lake, Michelle Corral, Juanita Bynum, Oral Roberts, Corrie Ten Boom, Aimee Semple McPherson, TD Jakes and Sid Roth.

It all begins with a few coming together and praying powerfully! If you do not have powerful prayer warriors in your home or your group of friends, yet, you can begin by joining with the greats while listening to the You Tube videos, watching and hearing the testimonies of the mighty men & women of God.

Kathryn Kuhlman TV interviews with such greats as Corrie Ten Boom and Sid Roth are easily found on You Tube. Their testimonies will bless you! Plus, Kathryn's meetings at Oral Roberts University. Aimee Semple McPherson, Michelle Corral and Juanita Bynum testimonies and programs on You Tube are amazing. Aimee's videos include amazing details about progress in the lives of people in Hollywood during it's golden years with the meetings resulting in the launch of missionaries globally within a very short time of their salvation. Powerful details and examples.

Testimony regarding **Sid Roth** blessing many which changed the life of a husband and wife forever! A man shared a testimony about listening to a Sid Roth radio broadcast within a local bible study. His life changed when he heard a caller ask Sid: *How can I be filled with the Holy Spirit?* Sid asked the man to repeat his words. The man repeated the Holy Spirit language as Sid prayed and he was filled and blessed. Plus, the man sharing this testimony was listening to the program and he was filled and deeply blessed! His wife told him that he could do it if he wanted to but, per her church belief she wanted none of it. He told her that was great because he wanted all of it. Within a short time frame, after she observed what the LORD was doing in her husband's life, she asked him to tell her about the radio broadcast, again. He did and he began speaking in tongues. His wife repeated what he said. Within moments, she began speaking and praying in tongues & she was mightily blessed!

Who will the LORD send into your life to impact your life? Who has He sent to you ... people you did not 'impact' at the time because you did not know how? Seek & find them. Then, bless them with the truth! What impact will your words and actions have on the people in your life? Please share the testimonies far & wide. Plus, send details to us in an email to hisbest4usorders@gmail.com which includes *Always Speak Life* in the subject line. Thanks!

Chapter 5   Our Words Have Power!

Perhaps a good visual would help: A person (maybe you, maybe me) being encouraged, inspired and restored when words are spoken or being diminished, defeated or destroyed due to the words spoken. Our words have power!

The scripture on the cover of the book was changed from the first part of **Proverbs 18:21.** *Death and life are in the power of the tongue* the same day the cover was submitted for approval.

The LORD provided a replacement scripture to insert and He only wanted me to include the first half, the positive half: *For the eyes of the LORD are on the righteous, and His ears are open to their prayers ...* **I Peter 3:12.** The rest of the verse: *But the face of the LORD is against those who do evil.* Wow, that's an eye opener!

We often hear only the first part of the verse quoted. It is the same for **Proverbs 18:21**: *Death and life are in the power of the tongue* but, the rest of the verse is not quoted: *And those who love it will eat its fruit.* Plus, it would be powerful for us to know and repeat the prior verse: *A man's stomach shall be satisfied from the fruit of his mouth; from the produce of his lips he shall be filled.*

Wow. Our words have power to satisfy and fill us or destroy us and each person we speak about or talk to or about each day. Wow.

Our words have power!

Typically, I am asked to pray first for all of the people who are experiencing health problems, especially when the church bulletins are focused upon a list of prayer requests for the dis-eases the people in the host congregation are experiencing.

Often, family members tell me they are very concerned about prayers which appear to 'build up hope', the hope that their loved ones are going to live especially if they are going to die.

Wow. What has happened to us?

When we come to Christ, we have life in Christ!

Important to shift our focus, now: Life in Christ gives us 'life on earth and in heaven' which is a great gift. The LORD promises a hope and a future, He does not promise tomorrow to any of us!

Prayer theme: *Always Speak Life.*

Why? Our words have power!

Two key issues we have to deal with regarding our words.

1. For the people experiencing dis-ease. Unforgiveness and becoming 'positioned' regarding a situation which means we are unwilling to repent. **Psalms 130:3-5.** *If you, LORD, should mark iniquities, O LORD, who could stand? But, there is forgiveness with You, that You may be feared* (respected). *I wait for the LORD, my soul waits, and in His word I do hope.* II **Chronicles 7:14.** *If My people who are called by My name will humble themselves, and pray and seek My face, and turn from their wicked ways, then I will hear from heaven, and will forgive their sin and heal their land.*

Mark 11:25. Forgiveness and Prayer. *And whenever you stand praying, if you have anything against anyone, forgive him, that your Father in heaven may also forgive you your trespasses.*

Psalms 32:1. The Joy of Forgiveness. *Blessed is he whose transgression is forgiven, whose sin is covered.* **Psalms 106:1.** *Praise the LORD! Oh, give thanks to the LORD, for He is good! For his mercy endures forever.*

Psalms 39:1. Prayer for Wisdom and Forgiveness. I said, *I will guard my ways, lest I sin with my tongue; I will restrain my mouth with a muzzle, while the wicked are before me.*

2. For the people praying who spread the details person to person which confirm dis-ease vs. healing, spreading gossip:

Proverbs 16:28. *A perverse man sows strife, and a whisperer separates the best of friends.*

I Timothy 5:13. *And besides they learn to be idle, wandering about from house to house (or calling in modern times), and not only idle but also gossips and busybodies, saying things which they ought not.*

This is what happens when we align with the enemy and speak about the list of dis-eases. We repeat the words which are clearly without hope. Important Reminder: Remember who we are in Christ! We are promised a hope and a future!

II Corinthians 2:14-17. Now thanks be to God who always leads us in triumph in Christ, and through us diffuses the fragrance of His knowledge in every place. For we are to God the fragrance of Christ among those who are being saved and among those who are perishing. To the one we are the aroma of death leading to death, and to the other the aroma of life leading to life. And who is sufficient for these things? For we are not, as so many, peddling the word of God; but as of sincerity, but as from God, we speak in the sight of God in Christ.

Life in Christ means: Our words have power!

When we pray, we either speak Life (Christ) or Death (aligning with the enemy).

Acts 26:18-19. being sent by God: t*o open their eyes, in order to turn them from darkness to light, and from the power of Satan to God, that they may receive forgiveness of sins and inheritance among those who are sanctified by faith in Me.*

Our words have power!

Have you ever heard *Upside Down* by Lou Rawls?

If not, you can find it on You Tube. Check it out. You will enjoy it, I promise!

During a very special time in my life, I was dating a man with two children, a son and a daughter: Jay was 10 and Lori was 7 when I met them.

When we met, they were not excited about very much in their life. So, on the days when I was asked to help them get to school or to an after school activity, I kept the tape of *Upside Down* handy.

At the time, I was driving a Nissan Z coupe because I enjoyed high speed rallies on California mountain routes, so one of them had to squeeze into the very small back seat area which would cause some teasing and sometimes a brief smile.

Early morning did not automatically result in a smile.

So, I started a new 'procedure' as soon as they were in the car. I slipped the *Upside Down* song into the tape deck without saying a word. The routine took a while to sink in. Adding a donut stop at Peterson's Bakery became a routine which helped the process the first few days. Within a couple of days, their smiles appeared as soon as they heard the music. Over time, they learned the song and sang along with Lou. It was adorable. The best news was: It changed their attitude about their day and their life!

If you have not started listening to *Upside Down* yet, please click on one of the options within You Tube right now.

Don't worry, after you have listened to the words, I'll be waiting for you right here.

The message is so clear. A few examples:

Everybody has an upside.

Everybody's got a downside.

If you start to feel a down slide you can turn it around.

There's a million things you can do ...

Don't let anything or anybody turn your upside down.

If you're feeling good you know you shouldn't let them turn you around.

There's a million things you can do ...

Just go on your way, go on with your day.

Don't let anything or anybody turn your upside down.

This is true about our words, also. With help from our LORD, we will know what the people are in pain about and our prayers will become powerful and significant in their life.

We either encourage or discourage people because each of our words truly have an upside or a downside.

Take a moment to think about our LORD, imagine how our LORD feels when he hears 'all of it' especially since He already knows everything we know about 'it' and everything else we do not know, yet, about 'it'.

Our words have power!

This is why it is so important for us to *Always Speak Life.*

When people invite me to their events or to their homes, I often hear repetitive prayers. When Christ gave us the 'model prayer' he warned us to speak directly with our LORD; He confirmed we are to meet Him in private, in secret for He is in the secret places with us, and then speak to Him out of our relationship with Him.

Matthew 6:7-8. And <u>when you pray, do not use vain repetitions as the heathen *do*. For they think that they will be heard for their many words.</u> [8] <u>Therefore do not be like them. For your Father knows the things you have need of before you ask Him.</u>

There is a shift which takes place when we stop repeating the exact words, calling them prayers when we say the same words when we wake up, when we begin a meal or before we go to bed.

While I was growing up, I learned amazing words, prayers I repeated the exact same way during each part of the day. Trusting I'm not the only one who learned: *Now I lay me down to sleep, I pray the LORD my soul to keep; If I should die before I wake, I pray the LORD my soul to take.* It will forever be in my memory bank.

It's different regarding the lunch time prayer, however. Each time I returned to my family home for a visit, it became harder and harder for me to remember any of the words of the the prayer stated by my family as soon as everyone was seated around the kitchen table for breakfast, lunch or dinner.

Being away from home and family resulted in different prayers being spoken before each meal and yet, the LORD had to reveal the truth to me. I used to ask a list of people to pray with me. I thought they were all going to pray powerful prayers on my behalf. I never considered the fact they would ever speak against my request or think it is not possible for the LORD to resolve the problem or the situation I was facing!

The LORD merely told me to stop asking them when He prompted me to pray with them while we were together, instead. I was shocked to hear their words. In most cases, they actually apologized and told me the situation(s) would not improve and they shared details about the many times the LORD has not answered similar prayers for them. So, feeling defeated, they actually aligned with the enemy instead of standing in faith and hope for my future, the promise we each have from our LORD!

Lord, thank you for loving us, for keeping your hand upon us, remaining close and guiding us each step of the way while giving us the words in the moment while we are together with believers and non-believers so Your will will be done. May we become a testimony of our relationship with You which will draw people closer and closer to You each time we speak with them or pray with them.

Chapter 6   Power Of Prayer

What are the top ten reasons to be grateful, to give thanks?

1.

2.

3.

4.

5.

6.

7.

8.

9.

10.

Each morning, this is the place to begin the day, and then, living your life 'on top of' your top ten reasons to be grateful and give the LORD thanks'! Powerful place to begin. Just sayin' … !

Over time, we can easily fall into 'petition prayers' and repetitive prayers and stay there the rest of our life.

Sad but, true.

How does this happen? We know our LORD loves us and we often hear: **John 15:7.** *If you abide in Me, and My words abide in you, you shall ask what you desire, and it shall be done for you.*

Well, now we know how to abide with our LORD, spend time with Him and speak with Him from our heart!

What is the 'thing' you think God should do for you?

Everywhere I go, people crowd the prayer line with a request for God to do one more thing.

Survey says: Fix a family member (often # 1) or deposit cash into an account (typically #1 or # 2). God has provided it all but, in your mind, what is the one 'thing' that you are holding out hope for, something else for God to do?

What if the dead 'thing' in our life could be fixed without God having to do one more 'thing' for us?

What if we spoke LIFE vs. DEATH about our dead 'thing'?

God's Pure Religion

I agree with the sentiment ... we need to stop being religious, we really, really need to give it up! But, we need to do it ONLY because of what we have turned religion into! We changed it!

His pure religion: <u>Care for the widows</u> (which have expanded to become all women without husbands) <u>and orphans</u> (which have expanded to become all children without fathers), **James 1:27,** <u>and keep ourselves unspotted from the world.</u>

Pray for them. Seek the LORD for ways & sources to bless them. Then, be in action about what the LORD reveals to you!

Widows

Spend time seeing to the needs of the widows and mothers without husbands, and share your blessings, sources and resources so they will be blessed.

Often, a list of the needs (handyman, auto repairs, medical exams, legal review of issues, etc.) and a list of the tithe of all skills, talents, abilities, products and services within the fellowship will be an exact match so all shall be blessed. Trusting the LORD seeds the fellowship with His provision for each of the needs.

Plus, the widows are not typically wage earners who would be tithing as their pension is based upon funds from which they already tithed. The tithe (all of who we are, more than just money) is supposed to be what is shared with the homeless, the widows and orphans, and then, based upon the 'increase' the people bring a portion of it to share the blessings.

It was a privilege to become a witness to the blessing granted to seven widows at Jubilee Church in Camarillo, California. The LORD told the leadership the exact number of widows and the blessing to prepare for each one the week prior to the service.

During the service, the widows were asked to come forward and prayers continued until the seventh widow joined the women in front of the church. Then, a stack of crisp $100 bills were handed to each one. It was the first time the widows were blessed by a church.

Orphans

Visit the orphanages and help any way possible to empty the orphanages so the children will learn the truth before they become adults.

Proverbs 22:6. *Train up a child in the way he should go, and when he is old he will not depart from it.*

God wants us to see to the needs of the orphans.

This is part of what He asks of me in each region where He places my feet. Much can be learned by checking on the welfare of the children instead of merely enjoying a pleasant community tour. Most orphanages will only let you see the facility, not the children.

Please be persistent to pray before you go, pray while you are there and do all you can to see how it is with the children.

Example: God told me to go to a local orphanage for the sake of a young lady. I only knew her first name.

Since I did not have a car, the LORD told me to call a pastor and ask him for a ride to attend a prayer meeting at his church. A house parent from the orphanage was in attendance so, I trusted he was my way to get to the orphanage.

He was not since he did not have a car. However, he did make arrangements for me to meet with the young girl during lunch on Saturday. I just had to secure a ride to the orphanage and before the prayer meeting was over, God made all the arrangements.

Orphanage: 11:30 AM, Saturday. House mother was still asleep. The young lady, Lauren, invited me into her room. She showed me a few of her drawings: Satan and Angels.

She said she was ready to go to heaven so God could make her an angel and give her wings. Then, she would be able to go where God needs her to go to help because she is restricted to her class room and her bed room on earth.

She was not able to get a second chance from any of the adults, so, she trusted Baal & the Queen of Heaven (she was told the Queen is Mary, the mother of Christ). They wanted her to do this so she could negotiate with God for the fallen angels, the Nephilim, so they could get a second chance.

The enemy is working diligently with the youth, and especially the orphans!

We prayed for the non-believing teacher & administrator of the children's home (orphanages are now wanting to be called children's homes). When I returned to my temporary hosting location, the LORD asked me to Google the home and study the information.

I cried out to the LORD for a car so I could go to the school & to the home to meet with the non-believing teacher, the social worker for the home & the administrator.

At the same time, a woman I had not met heard the LORD tell her to: *"...donate the car* (she moved to another state a couple of weeks prior & left a car on her driveway) *to the woman your parents have told you about for several months* (nine)*, because she needs to go where I need her to go instead of where people are willing to take her."*

With keys in hand by Thursday morning, I asked the LORD for confirmation: *"Should I drive to the school or the home?"*

God merely whispered, ***"I've got this!"***

The next Sunday, Lauren wanted to give a testimony.

She kept pointing at me, saying: *"That woman was told by God to come and see me because I am special to Him. She said* (Lauren then stated many quotes from our brief meeting, clearing up who Baal is and who the Queen of Heaven is, being a joint heir vs. an angel, etc.) *and on Thursday morning my teacher said: 'I never give a second chance but, I am supposed to give you a second chance ... never clear your record ... but, I'm supposed to for you ... '* Everything was cleared up & her rights were restored.

Two weeks later, Lauren had a new testimony. Her mom left her at the home 18 months before due to not having an income. Lauren said she learned how to pray from her heart during our brief meeting. So, she prayed on behalf of her mom each day & her mom got a job!

Blessed And Highly Favored

How did it used to feel when you were in the midst of a crisis and the people around you were saying they are blessed and highly favored? If you are going to share this status with people, please be willing to be with them, listen to them from your heart and pray with them regarding the situation(s) and issue(s) they are facing.

Important to remember when you were in crisis, you were not feeling favored. And, when we are not feeling favored, we are absolutely not feeling favored. Can I get an AMEN?

Now that the 'state of being human' is known, I can share the secret: Life in Christ means we are blessed and highly favored.

Go ahead and breathe.

Think about the people the LORD sent into your path and ask Him what can be done to bless them, express the LORD's truth to them and help them realize they are blessed and chosen by God.

Take another good, deep breath and breathe in the truth with the next breath of life with them! That way, the blessings will flow one to another and hopefully from your heart from this day forward! This is my hope for your future!

The scriptures are true. When David felt he was not being heard, **Psalms 22:1-2,** *My God, My God, why have You forsaken me? Why are You so far from helping Me, And from the words of My groaning? O My God, I cry in the daytime, but You do not hear; And in the night season, and am not silent.*

Then, David reminded himself of the truth: **Psalms 22:3.** *But You are holy, enthroned in the praises of Israel.*

John 6:63. It is the Spirit who gives life; the flesh profits nothing. The words that I speak to you are spirit, and *they* are life.

For the eyes of the Lord are on the righteous, and His ears are open to their prayers ... **1 Peter 3:12**

I Corinthians 2:9. ... Eye has not seen, nor ear heard, nor have entered into the heart of man the things which God has prepared for those who love Him.

Romans 8:37-39. Yet in all these things we are more than conquerors through Him who loved us. [38] For I am persuaded that neither death nor life, nor angels nor principalities nor powers, nor things present nor things to come, [39] nor height nor depth, nor any other created thing, shall be able to separate us from the love of God which is in Christ Jesus our Lord.

Whatever we face: **Count it all joy!**

James 1:2-6. Profiting from Trials. My brethren, count it all joy when you fall into various trials, [3] knowing that the testing of your faith produces patience. [4] But let patience have *its* perfect work, that you may be perfect and complete, lacking nothing. [5] If any of you lacks wisdom, let him ask of God, who gives to all liberally and without reproach, and it will be given to him. [6] But let him ask in faith, with no doubting, for he who doubts is like a wave of the sea driven and tossed by the wind.

Chapter 7   Take Dominion And Authority

Challenged every time I talk about us standing up to the elements, taking dominion and authority.

However, from the very moment we were formed in God's image, we were given dominion:

Genesis 1:26b-28. ... *over the fish of the sea, over the birds of the air, and over the cattle and over every creeping thing that creeps on the earth. So God created man in His own image; in the image of God He created him; male and female He created them. Then, God blessed them, and God said to them, "Be fruitful and multiply; fill the earth and subdue it; have dominion over the fish of the sea, over the birds of the air, and over every living thing that moves on the earth."*

I'm also questioned about being a woman taking authority however, the LORD created us in his image, male and female.

Ah, the LORD provides the truth. We merely have to seek His truth.

And, the truth is in the answers when the LORD knows we are in relationship with Him, seeking His will and asking what He has need of us to do on this day and then we do it! That is the key.

Having faith and thinking we can do it is nice but, as we are reminded in **James 2** faith without works, taking action, is dead. We must speak the truth and be obedient to act upon the truth.

Example: It was a stormy afternoon when I received the urgent, panic phone call: *Tell me how to take dominion and authority over the storm headed directly to my home!*

Panic had already set in.

Sister of a dear friend was having a new roof installed on her family home. The workers wanted to stop because they were seeing powerful lightning strikes in the distance, especially upsetting to them from their roof top perspective.

The roof was only half finished.

The supervisor just reminded the owner of her choice to not pay for an insurance policy in case of rain damage.

Therefore, all water damage would become her responsibility, her expense.

This was her first phone call after she heard me speak during an afternoon session about our powerful position in prayer: taking dominion and authority.

It is important to be specific, so I asked a few questions while I also guided her through the prayer, step by step. It's more powerful and it helps us learn what we need to say when we pray the words, assisted while taking a firm stand to pray through our own situations!

We started our prayer by thanking the LORD for removing the lightning and all affects from the storm, now.

The lightning strikes stopped along with the removal of the related thunder.

This gave the men on the roof a little peace of mind and it strengthened her resolve in praying through.

Then, I asked for her address.

While we prayed and thanked the LORD for full protection of her address, I trusted she had a home with a front and back yard while the details did not matter so long as we confirmed the right address.

We thanked the LORD for holding back the rain from the north, south, east and west of her exact property address.

Then, I asked her how long the men needed to be on the roof to finish their work. The supervisor confirmed if the rain did not reach her property, they could be done by 3:30 PM. So, that is what we thanked the LORD for, keeping the rain away from her property address until after 3:30 PM.

The rain was quickly approaching her home by the time we finished the prayer. She confirmed all details with the Supervisor before we ended the call.

One week later, I called her sister to obtain the testimony because no urgent call was received to rejoice because the LORD answered each and every request.

Lord help us share the truth of our testimony far & wide.

Rain fell on all land around the <u>five acres</u> of her property!

No rain fell on her property while the men were on the roof.

The work was done by 3:30 PM. When the Supervisor got in his truck at 3:31, the rain was fully released on her property!

We do serve an awesome God, a LORD who wants us to be in relationship with Him, praying with Him especially as two or more who will come together with Christ being in the midst with us while we seek the LORD's will in our life.

Before I took power and authority, the LORD did it all!

If you are concerned about having someone available to walk through the process with you, stop. Surrendering all, becoming available for the will of the LORD to be done is all He asks.

Seven days the LORD kept the gas tank full. I was obedient, I did all the LORD asked of me. I was offered a blessing beyond the rental car and gas. However, the man who was going to bless me left town without sharing the blessing. The LORD has confirmed again and again that His plans are true and the world plan may not unfold.

When it was time for me to drive from the north end of California back to San Diego, the tank was empty and the rental car bill was due. I was not happy! The LORD listened to my complaints half the way South of the 5 Freeway while the truth was evident: the LORD filled the tank and kept it full!

The LORD kept the tank full for seven days, which included driving hundreds of miles.

The Provision of the LORD was given by His taking power and authority over my situation.

As often as I complained about 'not having enough gas' … the LORD kept the gas tank full until His provision was 'in hand'.

He sent a man with an envelope of money to provide the blessing and pay the rental car fees.

Where there seems to be no way, the LORD makes a way!

Standing in awe about the gas tank to this very day and it was after a series of divine orchestrations which are beyond human comprehension.

When I was sent to re-encourage a pastor, he informed me I needed to get a ticket to be in Australia in three days. It was a faith building experience. I used one of his office phones and his staff heard my faith-building experience.

Each airline employee said, *"It will take a miracle to get you there..."* caused me to build my faith with each response when God confirmed, *"Great, because I live based on miracles."* The woman who granted the ticket wanted to hear more details about God needing me to be in Australia within three days. She set up a meeting with the American Airlines & Qantas employees in Los Angeles, when my San Diego flight connected to the direct flight to Sydney, Australia.

In Search of Wigglesworth: A messenger was sent by the LORD to give me the clue: go to the library to find the mural of Wigglesworth.

After, the LORD woke up a teenager to prepare the mural about Wigglesworth after I accepted the assignment to search for Wigglesworth.

After, the LORD directed the teen to provide the exact clue needed: Sunderland.

After, the LORD sent a specific taxi driver for us who was baptized in Wigglesworth's church, so he would also be blessed by the journey ...

There are merely a few of the many divine orchestrations which caused me to stand in awe on the seven day journey.

God continues to do it: The LORD orchestrated the book *God's Currency* in seven days. *In Search of Wigglesworth* was adjusted from a chapter within *It's A Faith Walk* to a separate book with a specific purpose in seven days. *In One Accord* was completely restructured and adjusted to become what the LORD wanted it to be in seven days and this book, *Always Speak Life,* was completely structured, re-structured and adjusted within the last seven days.

The LORD would not do it for Paul Cain and not do it for me!

The LORD sent Paul Cain to speak into the life of Saddam Hussein. Then, between the airport and the palace, the car stopped in the middle of the desert. The driver opened the hood and showed Paul and Saddam the hole which was created by a rock going through the engine. Saddam told Paul he needed to pray to his God since his God sent him to give the word and it would not be good if his God let him die in the desert.

Paul prayed! At the appropriate time, Paul told the driver to turn the key. In that moment, the car started and they drove on to a mechanic the driver knew in the town where the palace was located. The mechanic was puzzled when he heard the 'story' because there was no hole in the engine. When the driver, Paul & Saddam looked at the engine, they knew the LORD Paul served had 'healed' the engine as it was in perfect condition!

Paul Cain shared this testimony the day the LORD said He was sending me to Africa, seven months prior to the trip the LORD arranged within three weeks.

Africa trip was arranged by the LORD within three weeks, after I was not able to put the details together in seven months, an accomplishment which is impossible 'in the natural'.

The last night of 'the gas tank being full', the LORD arranged for me to meet again with the man being crowned king in Africa in three weeks. The LORD gave him a word for me and yet, the man ran out of time to deliver the word. The LORD kept prompting me to tell him I will be in Ghana, and he can give me the word in Africa. In fact, the promptings were so persistent, I said 'out loud': *I'm not going to Ghana.* The LORD convicted my heart the moment I was in the rental car & He arranged all funds & details to be in Africa within three weeks. Not one dime for the trip touched my hands!

My prayer for us: May we choose to become a living testimony in our daily life. May we declare to all what our LORD does for us. May each prayer and request glorify the Father through the Son!

Lord we thank you for making us in your image, giving us dominion to operate in power and authority on earth, praying aligned with Your will, blessing the people with the truth so the body of Christ will come into one accord, functioning and operating together as the body of Christ on earth!

Personal Note 'Just Between Us'

Within a very short time, our Savior, the true Messiah, Jesus Christ, Yeshua Hamashiach, accomplished everything He came to earth to accomplish!

He confirmed we would do the things He did & greater. What are we accomplishing which glorifies the Father through the Son?

Now that you know the potential of your life in Christ, what will the LORD do through you during the next few weeks and months? I look forward to hearing the details!

Praying and trusting that now, since you are armed with the truth and you realize how powerful we are in Christ, you will be willing to pray powerfully for your situation(s) and issue(s) and the situation(s) and issue(s) of the people the LORD sends to you!

Remember, when you walk in the truth guided by the Holy Spirit, it's easy to know what to do since the adventures laid out before you are divinely orchestrated by the LORD!

God knows me so well! The good news (perhaps the best news) is: The LORD knows everything about you, also!

God does not love any one of us even an ounce more.

When someone knows something or has a gift we do not have, we tend to think they have a closer relationship or they are loved more than we are loved by God but, the LORD loves each and every one of His children for His desire is for each of us to prosper as our soul prospers!

The truth is, we <u>each</u> serve an awesome God who loves each of us. Here's to you and all the plans He has laid out before you!

May you take the LORD's hand and proceed with His wisdom while enjoying experiences which inspire, encourage and re-encourage you, your family, the people in your community and future generations! I look forward to hearing your testimonies! Until the next ONE MORE TIME our Lord brings us together may you continue to experience HIS Best!

Sheila

Email: hisbest4usorders@gmail.com
Use the Subject Line: **Always Speak Life**
Web site: http://hisbest4us.org
Facebook: HISBest4us

Ephesians 2:19-22 *We are no longer foreigners and aliens, but fellow citizens... members of God's household, built on the foundation of the apostles and prophets, with Christ Jesus himself as the chief cornerstone. In Him the whole building is joined together and rises to become a holy temple in the Lord. And in Him you too are being built together to become a dwelling in which God lives by His Spirit.*

II Corinthians 12:14-15. (a) *"Now, I am ready to visit you...what I want is not your possessions but you...So I will very gladly spend for you everything I have and expend myself as well."*

II Corinthians 13:11-14. *Aim for perfection ... be of one mind, live in peace, and the God of love and peace will be with you. May the grace of the Lord Jesus Christ, and the love of God, and the fellowship of the Holy Spirit be with you all.*

Books Authored by Sheila Holm

It's A Faith Walk!

February 15, 2014

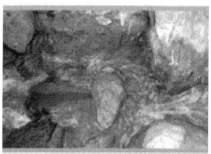

God's Storehouse Principle

March 26, 2014

Workbook for

God's Storehouse

Principle

April 4, 2014

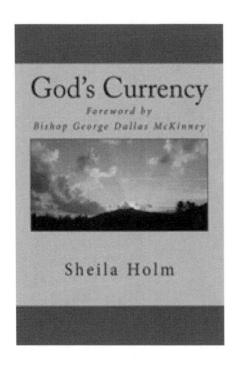

God's Currency

April 18, 2014

Nation Restoration

July 1, 2014

A Wake Up Call:

It's Restoration Time!

May 8, 2015

In Search of

Wigglesworth

September 23, 2015

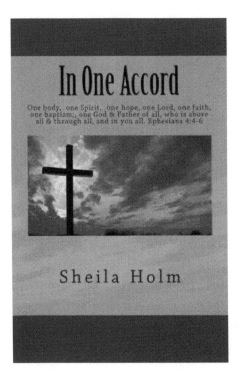

In One Accord

September 28, 2015

A Peculiar People

October 7, 2015

Seven Step

Business Plan

Published, 2007

Latin America edition:

Spanish Language

Published, 2009

ACKNOWLEDGMENTS

AFRICA

Ghana, West Africa

Pastor Sam,

"Truly, God has sent you to us with a strong word for our church."

Pastor Charles,

"It blesses my soul to hear of your faith & see the fruit of the ministry."

Johannesburg, South Africa
Pastor Jhanni,

"God is doing a good work through you and I pray with you & our church."

Coronation Ceremony

AMERICA

Dr. Nancy Franklin, Georgia

"Thank you God for answering my prayers by sending Your apostle to (the region) to unite the believers ... "

Prophetess Nancy Haney, Alaska

"God has never given me this before. I see circles and circles and circles ... you drink and you draw from one circle to the other, and that's what you do, you drink and draw and you bring these circles together ... Pulling many groups together.

All these groups need each other ... He can use you for you have ears to hear and you hear His deep truth. You are filtering what is nonsense and what is real ... because you have been in that circle, and because of what you say they are going to merge. It is going to expand, become bigger than you could imagine."

Pastor, Host of "Praise the Lord", TBN,

"...The fruit of the ministry is evident in your testimony..."

Man of God (Georgia), Requesting to be Discipled while attending the coronation of a King in Africa, Georgia

"...at my age, it is hard to believe I am learning so much in these few days about what I did not know...realizing what it is to know that I know how it is to live within God's word each day. Will you consider discipling me?"

International Prophet,

"You have remained steadfast to God's plan and God will continue to send you forth for His plan and purpose to be fulfilled, and for the thousands who have not knelt..."

President, Christian Publishing Company

"Only God could orchestrate such a grand plan..."

Prayer Director, International Prayer Center

"God is opening many doors for you..."

Christian Publisher, **"God has given you a powerful voice and a sweet spirit..."**

Pastor, Southern California

"God is raising you up and sending you forth to many nations..."

International Apostle

"God is doing a mighty work through you, for His righteousness precedes you, showers over you and follows you as a mighty wake. May it continue for each of your days..."

Prophetic Prayer Partner, Minnesota

"Only God could walk you through these days... accomplish so much through you, in the midst of your daily situations, the many blessings shared during each of your travels will continue to shower blessings upon each of the many households around the world..."

AUSTRALIA

Newcastle, New South Wales, Australia

*Pastor Mark, "...***the staff and business leaders heard the message of Personal &Professional Life Management this week, so we are blessed you agreed to preach the word to our church this morning."**

Four Square Gospel Church, Aboriginal Cultural Center

*Pastor Rex, "***God blessed us through your preaching on Easter Sunday. We will never forget that you were in our midst ... God brought new people to Jesus today & we thank God for what He has done because you answered His call."**

Prayer Team Meeting **"We know now how we will we be able to continue this mighty work when you are not in our midst..."**

ENGLAND

London, England

Pastor Vincent, Glory House, East London,

> *"...the honor is ours this Easter Sunday."*

Associate Pastor,

> **"The Glory of our God Almighty shines upon you and through you in your speaking and your actions...we give Him praise."**

Protocol Team,

> **"God has mightily blessed us, by sending you into our midst."**

Pastor Arnold,

> **"You have blessed the people of this congregation, and in His wisdom and timing, may He bring you back into our midst again, very soon."**

Pastor, West London,

"We rejoice with you in hearing and seeing the mighty things God is doing."

Pastor, South London, "Our God is evidenced in your life and your speaking, while we continue to thank God for the work He is doing through you..."

High Commissioner, Kingdom of Tonga, serving in the Embassy in London, England; Ambassador Akosita, "God's timing is always right...for you to be with us, prior to the Economic Summit, to meet and pray with us..."

Sunderland, England

Anglican, Former Church of Pastor Smith Wigglesworth

Pastor Day, **"I thank God for sending you to our church this morning, for serving communion to me, and for renewing and restoring me for the call upon my life."**

Kingdom of TONGA

Pastor Isileli Taukolo, "**Our board and business leaders were fasting and praying and God confirmed He was sending someone to us. We are deeply touched by the message God sent to us, through you.**"

Minister of Finance, Tasi, "**Our meeting was an answer to my prayers, and I thank you for providing the seminar for our senior staff members, and meeting with them individually for prayer and coaching.**"

Government Office, "**Thank you for speaking today and for staying and praying with us.**"

Interpreter, Sela

About the Author

The LORD fulfills upon His promises within the scriptures. He has equipped and trained Sheila while He:

- Places her feet on the soil of every continent,
- Sends her forth without an extra coin or tunic,
- Arranges flights and accommodations in each nation,
- Introduces her before she arrives,
- Lifts her up and encourages her,
- Seats her before governors and kings,
- Fills her as an empty vessel,
- Shares His wisdom and word of knowledge,
- Blesses and heals the people in her path,
- Comforts and re-encourages her to encourage pastors, prophets, believers, teachers & evangelists,

- Touches people individually in conferences/multitude,
- Speaks through her with power and authority,
- Takes people into gift of laughter when she preaches,
- Addresses situations the body of Christ is facing,
- Unites the people in the region,
- Confirms His word through her with each prayer & message shared,
- Speaks through her so people hear His words in their own language, especially when the translators also experience the gift of laughter and stop translating.

- Directs her path to speak life into each situation whether God sends people to her to be re-encouraged or he asks her to pray with a pastor, the church, or someone in a store or a restaurant, etc.

God has taken Sheila around the globe, church to church, business to business, nation to nation.

Many confirm she walks in the five-fold ministry. She does not use a title because God does the work while He sends her as an apostle and prophet and He orchestrates all arrangements for her to preach, teach, and evangelize.

People attending the conferences often say her segments are like watching someone walk out of the bible, share for a while and then, go right back in the bible, aka continue upon her journey in HIStory.

Made in the USA
Columbia, SC
24 February 2024

31973449R00043